CW01433386

21 INSIGI

Authentic

L I V I N G

CHERLENE WILSON

CW
CHERLENE
WILSON

Copyright © 2017 by Cherlene Wilson Ltd

All rights reserved. Written permission must be secured from the publisher to use or reproduce any part of this book, except for brief quotations in critical reviews or articles.

Publisher: Cherlene Wilson Publishing House
Photography: Nargis Cross Photography
Book Cover Design: Cherlene Wilson Studios
Distributed by: Cherlene Wilson Publishing House

IBSN: 978-1542543897

Dedication

21 Insights for Authentic Living is dedicated to the memory of my father – Mr Mc Gregor Whittingham Wilson and my entire family.
To those near and those far and the ones who are yet to come. I love you!

CONTENTS

About the Author

CHERLENE WILSON is a London born, multi-faceted woman who believes 'boxes were created for things not people' and as such every individual ought to make it their quest in life to fully understand their uniqueness.

She attended Middlesex University receiving an associates degree psychology and criminology and has a 5 year diploma from Bethel School of Supernatural Ministry in Redding, California.

Cherlene is CEO of Cherlene Wilson Ltd and Co-Founder of The Nia Nzuri Foundation in Ghana, West Africa. Cherlene by profession is a certified Personality Analyst, Success Coach and International Speaker to men and women of influence across the globe. She is known to raise self-awareness, remove growth delaying blockages and ignite transformation, so that people can live confidently in the power of their identity, leverage their influence and increase their profits.

As a Personality Analyst she runs workshops in companies, schools and faith-based organisations, bringing clarity on how individuals are wired, to encourage self-acceptance, to understand themselves, enhance interpersonal skills and maximise their performance.

She has coached CEO's, leaders and celebrities to success in the confidence they feel today and is widely regarded as a "straight-talking, authentic and passionate coach". She is a trained Inner Healing Practitioner (SOZO, Bethel, Redding, California) bringing emotional wholeness to clients.

Cherlene's speaking engagements have spanned across the United States, South America, Canada, the Caribbean, U.K and Africa. She has spoken in educational institutions, rehabilitation/youth offending centres, correctional facilities, faith-based events and has been interviewed on numerous occasions for radio & television.

In her spare time Cherlene is deciding between being a vegan, vegetarian or pescatarian. She loves to travel, salsa dance, watch true stories and write. She has been seen in TV shows, commercials, on the stage (theatre) and film. She is also known for powerful spoken word poetry, has a cat called Blacks and believes that the stiletto is God's ultimate accessory given to women!

Connect with Cherlene - CherleneWilson.com | Facebook | Instagram | Periscope | Twitter - @cherlenewilson

Acknowledgements

This book exists because of the incredible people whose paths I have been honoured to cross. I would like to thank the number one lady in my life, my mother Beverley "don't-you-darling-me" Robinson. Your support has been unwavering, I'm eternally grateful to you, thank you - I love you. I would like to thank two of my mentors, Sheri Downs and Bernadette Ooley who walked along side me in my darkest moments and removed the lies I believed about myself and gave me permission to shine. I am grateful to my 'sista-friends' Steffany "oh my stars!" Gretzinger and Emilia K . Fuller who taught me what it looks like to fully be yourself, fully vulnerable, how to embrace process and be strong all at the same time - thanks loves!

To my besties: Noreen Mak'Osewe - thank you for the encouragement to write this book. The manifestation of this is pretty much because of you. You inspire me with your strength and tenacity to pursue dreams and leave here empty. Thank you for believing in me.

Lauren Evans - girl! "You may not always be there when I call, but you're always on time." From Day One with lipstick colour, a conference and flights across the pond, you embraced my "cray cray!" You are one of my biggest cheerleaders in life and for that and your love, I'm grateful.

Jay Kamara-Frederick - you've seen me through this entire evolution so far. Thank you for being an example of courage and the importance of speaking your truth even if your voice shakes! Your authenticity is admirable. Ladies thank you for embracing my "cray-cray", balloon releasing event, tears, celebratory you-know-whats, running around the house in excitement and all - This book is our collective victory - I love you!

To Danny Silk, you are one of my heroes and I'm so grateful to have you as a mentor. Your resources and time have been invaluable to me. Thank you for your straight-talking, patience and wisdom from my "tore-up-from-the-floor-up" days at BSSM to the present day. Your belief in me astounds me.

I'd like to thank Anthony David King. Ant, can you believe it? From crying my eyes out in my early twenties because I had no clue what I was supposed to be doing with my life, to this life!? Wow! Thank you for being that constant friend in every season - I appreciate you.

To the team at Cherlene Wilson Ltd and everyone who helped with this book, thank you for your skills, support and love. To have you run along side me is such a beautiful thing! You are a gift that keeps on giving. I love each of you - eternal blessings to you.

Finally to my father, the late great Mc Gregor Whittingham Wilson who epitomised authenticity and principle in our family and who always said "I could write a book you know?" Well 'my dad', I hope this one makes you proud - your dream has lived on through me.

Foreword
by Anthony David King

As an innovator, I've been fortunate to work with some of the most brilliant creative minds, ventures and investors around the world for many years. From the streets of south London to the stars of Silicon Valley. With all of them, I am convinced one quality stands out head and shoulders above the rest. One characteristic seems to resonate not only with me but others more than any other: authenticity.

I've known Cherlene for many years. Longer than my mind wants to remember. Many know her as Cherlene Wilson, the successful personality analyst, success coach and international speaker. Others call her CeCie, I call her Cherls. I've also known her story for many years. I've been there over the time she's travelled the world in search of her true self. And I've been fortunate to be one of the few close friends in her life to share ideas with (we both get really excited by big ideas), there to give advice on what to do next, how to think about life, and often times to recommend a great life-changing book that might help on her journey of discovery.

Years later, I am humbled by two things: firstly, at the person Cherlene has become. The challenges she has battled through and overcome, to be who she is today is nothing short of a miracle. Her story is one of both inspiration and transformation. And secondly, to now be able to recommend another life changing book, to you. This one.

As you read *21 Insights for Authentic Living*, let its words resonate deep in your heart and mind knowing this: whatever life has thrown at you up to this point and beyond, that you are reading words from the heart and life of someone who understands, where you are, how you feel and exactly what it means to go through some of the most incredible challenges in life, to not give up and live to become a better and more authentic version of themselves.

The journey to discovering your authentic self is by no means an easy one. But few things in life are more worth it. And in this book, you have a roadmap that makes it easier. Because it is Cherlene's soul purpose to help you discover something in life only a few ever do - your authentic self.

- Anthony David King

Authors Note

"Authenticity is the daily practice of letting go of who we think we're supposed to be and embracing who we are".
- Dr Brené Brown

The most frequent comments I get on social media are "you are so authentic", and "you keep it real, that's why I watch/follow you". As a result, I have noticed my audience consists of many people who openly admire authenticity and who also have a desire to exhibit it.

Upon reflection, I wondered how I could help the self-confessed inauthentic individual and those who wouldn't dare tell anyone they were too. In my profession and social life, I have come across multitudes of people that have struggled to reveal their true identity. These individuals edit them-selves just to fit in. What I wanted to do, is pull together some anchor points, which I'll be calling 'insights', which have helped me practice authenticity daily.

It is my hope that we all win in the "show up wars" and bless our environments with our AWESOME-NESS! The world needs us! I mean…THANK GOD for Steve Jobs! Richard Branson and "Auntie" Oprah! They have blessed the world with their imagination and presence. We as a society get to benefit from the fruit of their lives! WE too can be THAT creative and influential, feeding people with our fruit. But first we must trust in the process of who we are continuously evolving into and allow our TRUE SELVES to be SEEN!

With no further ado and much love, enjoy!!

Introduction

"The whole point of being alive is to evolve into the complete person you were intended to be."
- Oprah Winfrey

I remember when living in-authentically was the default setting for my life. I would hide behind makeup, my fashion sense and a smile if I could be bothered to crack one. If people asked how I was, I'd reply with "I'm okay", when I fully well knew I was a BIG FAT LIAR!! Passive aggression was rife too. If I was upset about the way someone had treated me or something they'd said had hurt my feelings, my expression to them would be minimal. Cutting them off was the "best thing to do", right!? Errrmmm nooooo! All I was doing was avoiding conflict and being too cowardly about the situation to tell them how I really felt about it. Sound familiar?

Over time, I learnt that suppressing my "cray-cray" (both good and bad), thoughts, feelings and emotions, was causing harm to my soul. I would feel like no one "knew" me, and if no one knew me, how could their statement or actions that they liked/loved me be true? One day someone complimented me on how awesome they thought I was. I remember looking at them blank faced, and rolled my eyes (on the inside of course) thinking "If you really knew, you wouldn't say that". While in the middle of a "noooooobody-knows-me" tantrum in my head, I heard an internal voice say - "is it that nobody *knows* you, or is it that you have not been *showing* people who you are for them *to* know you?!"

Talk about a sucker punch to the gut! I mean...all that boo-hooing and blaming other people for their lack of interest, when the REAL issue wasn't with them at all, it was with me! I was the one failing to show up so they could "learn me", as my fellow Jamaican's would say!

After that epiphany back in 2008, the quest to be "known" became a practice - and let me tell you - it was not easy! In the beginning, most of my attempts would be marked with heart palpitations and curiosity if my friends would remain true, if the real Cherlene Samantha Wilson "stood up!"

Before I stepped away from the imposter to became the real me, I was highly unhappy with life and largely misunderstood. I would often label myself as boring and far from intelligent, not having a lot to offer in conversation. Listen - I've had "issues", high days and "deep-down-in-the-dumps" low days! I can be epically random, speak to myself, think WAY too deep at times and let's say....be rather "special", but I'm ok with that! If you know me or have been on my Periscope, you're probably chuckling because you know exactly what I mean!!!

Revealing your inner self and being honest without the fear of judgment can be daunting, can't it? We all desire love, connection and being "real", so it is natural to protect our hearts from negative responses and consequently suppress who we are. Especially in the era of modern technology we are currently in - we get sucked into presenting who we want the world to *think* we are because it's "safe".

Let's be honest here, sometimes it's terrifying to just...BE! Social media can make it all the more challenging. If we don't hold up our " shield against comparison", we will become susceptible to fabrication of the truth, hopelessness, envy, depression and "editing" ourselves for others.

Many of us are guilty (myself included in the past) of editing to "fit in" to what we think other people's expectations of us are. In all honesty how is that serving us?

"If you edit who you are it is highly probable that you will not fulfil the entirety of your purpose and destiny!"

You will come to learn (if you don't know already) I am extremely passionate about purpose and destiny! I want to help people peel back their layers, see who they really are and practically help them to become the best versions of themselves. I believe that everyone has a purpose on the planet, for many, more than one! Think about it for a moment, if one of your missions in life is to be a voice in the arts & entertainment industry, but you suppress, compare or edit who you are and what you have to offer, (i.e.. a way of thinking or skill set), how will you fulfil your specific purpose on earth and moreover - how will you reach the people that need exactly what you have to offer?

When I think of personalities such as Russell Brand and the somewhat controversial Kanye West, although what they say may not be liked by the masses, they seem to remain true to their core self. I may not personally agree with all they say or do, but I have a level of respect for them because of the courage I know it takes to just "be you" in the world. Sandi Krakowski is a person I greatly admire, (listed as one of Forbes' Top 20 Woman Social Media Influencers) as she unapologetically does an excellent job of presenting and expressing the gift she is to the world.

Darlings, it will take courage and process to break the practice of in-authenticity. It will take intentionality to remove the mask and keep it off. It will be a process to overcome the fear that often grips our hearts because we are afraid of judgement.

Some may say, "it's easy to be this person because I've been this person for so long and who I really am isn't much to write home about". That takes up SO much energy, doesn't it!? Let me ask you this - would you prefer to be falsely accepted by many as the person that you want people to believe you are, or be accepted by fewer, for who you really are? Practicing authenticity is necessary for our personal evolution. The freedom of our soul, the fulfilment of our dreams and truly experiencing a deep sense of love and belonging hinges on it.

If you happen to be someone who feels unknown and lonely, I know exactly how you feel. If you feel there is no one who cares to get to know you - I know exactly how that feels too! If you feel somewhat known, but still have challenges showing up in other areas, I've got you! And if you are "all the way real", and just want to see if there is anything you can glean from this book to maintain that, "Heeeeeeyyy! I see you boo!"

In *21 Insights for Authentic Living* I share some of the keys I've discovered in making authenticity a way of life. You are about to read the after-thoughts, practices and stories of experiences that have become anchors in keeping me true to myself and the world around me.

It is my heart-felt hope that somewhere in the lines of the following pages you'll be able to connect, think through, process and make steps towards living a more authentic life. It is my hope that the pages will serve you well and help you live in a place where all of who you are will be known.

Remember - you not only owe it to yourself to show up, but you also owe the world an encounter with your awesome self - #fact!

ONE

Looking at Your Darkness

"Your willingness to look at your darkness is what
empowers you to change."
- Iyanla Vanzant

Imagine it's night, you've just got home, rushing in
the house, neglecting turning the lights on because
you are desperate to get to the loo - we've all been
there right!? In that scenario, there are a couple of
things that typically happen in the absence of light:
firstly, your eyes begin to adjust to the darkness
and secondly, you trust familiarity to lead you to
where you are going. Now imagine as you find your
way, you hit your foot on something that causes
pain and slows you down, leaving you limping to the
'throne room'. It can be like that in our internal lives.
Many of us are fully aware of our darkness and

adjust to it. We navigate through life trusting our instinct to take us to where we want to go, occasionally bumping into situations or triggers that cause us pain from our past experiences.

In 2007, I went through what I refer to as the "darkest night of my soul". It consisted of months of depression as a result of a relationship where I was cheated on multiple times, and the shame of it kept me silent. The effects drastically impacted my emotional wellbeing, life seemed to be at a standstill. The internal darkness becoming so dense that even friends travelled across the city to visit me in an attempt to "snap me out" of it. The day came when I realised that looking inside and in turn confronting what was immobilising me was the only way I could break the disempowering cycle I had been living in. I had to accept the failure of the relationship and the "right for justice". Forgiveness was what essentially set me free.

That metaphoric darkness can be defined as anything, only you would truly know. Perhaps your inner critic, depression, substance misuse, anger, unfortunate life experience, denial or unforgiveness, sexual addictions etc. This darkness can become our "new normal" as we function through it the best we know how, even when we know we are at risk of bumping into our metaphoric obstacles along our way. It is critical that we remain honest with ourselves and those around us in order to live authentically. We must find courage if we are serious about showing up in the world as who we are meant to be so the people who need us can find us.

"We must find courage if we are serious about showing up in the world."

Darling, what is important to remember here is that darkness only exists in the absence of light. The key is for us to identify what that 'light' is and what we need to do to get it. It may be speaking to someone about what's going on, writing, dancing, receiving counselling, poetry, sports e.g.. boxing - yes boxing...the punching bag, ok?! I know...looking at our darkness is hard, especially when we want to ignore it; however it will be more soul destroying long term if we don't.

We must find courage to embrace the process, regardless of how scary or uncomfortable we may feel doing it. It may frighten you (if you haven't experienced it before), but I promise you, the feeling that comes when the soul is free is second to none.

As "auntie" Iyanla Vanzant says: "Our willingness to look at our darkness is what empowers us to change!" In my experience, I know I needed to make a decision, while keeping my faith in God and the people around me to assist me.The answer for who or what you need, to open up and be honest is right inside of you!

Let us be intentional to shed light in all areas of our soul and activate our power as we journey through this shared human experience called life.

My questions for you:

1. What are the dark places in your heart/life that you hide from?

2. What do you believe to be true about the areas of darkness?

3. How did those areas become the way they are? e.g.. ego, pride, events etc.

4. What can you do tomorrow that will give you courage to bring light to those places? i.e. forgiveness of self, forgiveness of others.

TWO

Own Your Truth, Own Your Story

"I have come to believe over and over again that what is most important to me must be spoken, made verbal and shared, even at the risk of having it bruised or misunderstood."
— Audre Lorde

To own one's truth takes the exploration, identification and acceptance of who they are. Owning our truth gives us the confidence to present ourselves as honouring our thoughts and personal convictions. In the beginning when I came to terms with this concept, it was scary putting my truth "out there" and saying "this is who I am, these are my thoughts and this is what I will stand for". Of course there was the fear of being misunderstood, teased even - which to be honest, happens from time to time, but that's ok. I mean think about it, do we understand everyone or why they hold to their truths? What is important to us, is important to us! We know the reasons those truths are ours, and that is what matters most. What is equally as important is the relationship we have with our hearts and choosing not to violate it, but rather honour its voice. Have you ever seen someone who has a strong conviction for something they believe in? Those people are admirable. 'A breath of fresh air' to behold, as we observe their unwavering stance in who they say they are and what they believe. In that same manner, when we hold true to our truths we will be that breath of fresh air and give permission for people to also be themselves.

Yes you may wonder if people will judge you, and frankly it will happen because people are people. But we must not let that stop us, even if our voice cracks, we sweat buckets or we get butterflies in our tummy, we must own it and speak it.

One of my convictions is to intentionally use my words to honour others, especially men. In my 'past life' I would dishonour them because of the experiences of my youth. As my 'evolved self', I now choose to use my words differently. Where I would have attempted to emasculate men and cut them down, I now encourage them. I'm extremely passionate about it, which has found me having Facebook and Periscope conversations to ladies about how powerful our words are to the men in our lives. One day I was invited to speak at a women's conference, as part of a panel for Q&A. A lady bravely asked a question - "What should I do about my husband who is not as intelligent as I would like him to be, and find particularly embarrassing at work functions when he engages in conversations with my colleagues?" It was a genuine, heartfelt question.

What happened next will forever be etched in my memory of what not to do...ever. The co-leader of the conference stood up and made a distasteful joke about the husband's intelligence (in his absence) that elicited uproars of laughter from people in the audience. I was shocked to my core. I gracefully took the

"Our truths set us apart. They breed an authenticity that people connect to."

microphone and said, "How is it, that we are at a conference that speaks about how we as women have treated men and need to change that, sit and laugh in the same breath at a very real situation where a women shares her heart about something she needs help with, and at the same time dishonour her husband? That, I would say is hypocritical and something that I do not find funny at all". You could hear a feather drop. The co-leader stood up and apologised for his conduct.

For me, what I said was not for applause, neither was it said for popularity. What I do know is, had I walked away from that day, having not said anything, to this day I would be kicking myself for not standing up for what I really believe in - honour.

Our truths set us apart. They breed an authenticity that people connect to. Rather than suppressing or hiding our story, let us learn how to identify the power in it. At fourteen years old I was groomed and raped (statutory) by a man who had influence in a church I attended. As a result I left the organisation, became a member of a gang, became more sexually active because in my mind sex equalled love. I took a few soft drugs and abused alcohol, attempted suicide at 15 and left school with one grade. In a turn of events when one of the guys in the gang was convicted for murder, things got serious very quickly. I knew life had to change so I attended college and started on the path to changing my life as I knew it.

As you can imagine there are so many aspects to the story (which I speak about in depth in an upcoming book available in early 2017) that I won't go into in this book. There has been twenty two years of process and healing, some extreme lows and some incredible highs. The most recent and notable high - organising a meeting with the man that abused me on 2nd of December 2016. I wanted to have an adult to adult conversation and share the impact that his actions had on my life year by year. It was important for me to have that conversation because I felt my voice had been muted after we had sex and he threatened me with "if you say anything to anyone you will be in trouble". By the time of the conversation I had claimed 90% of my voice, in speaking to him, it was me showing myself that I am powerful, I do have a voice and I can face any circumstance with confidence because I know who I am. That conversation gave me the 10% of my voice I had been missing.

For many years there was a lot of shame and degradation that I upheld over my life. For a number of years I didn't want to speak about it because I felt that I was a bad person and that people would judge me because of it. This happened until one day I realised that denying my story was only keeping me in a place of pain longer than I needed to be. I came to understand that I could own that story and redefine the message of it. No longer does the story have me hiding, but rather using it as a calling card to let people know - by example - that there is power in your story and it does not have to define you.

Owning our truth and owning our story is an integral part of our wholehearted existence. To not stand in your truth or suppress your story out of fear of the opinions of others, communicates that our fears have more power over us, but we can reverse that. We can reclaim the power of our story by being, honest, vulnerable and transparent in who we are and the things we have experienced.

My questions for you:

1. What part of your life story do you own?

2. What part of your life story do you not take ownership of?

3. What truths do you hold onto in life?

THREE

"Shame on Me?"

"The difference between shame and guilt is the difference between 'I am bad' and 'I did something bad'."
– Unknown

At the end of December in 2011 while living in Northern California, I visited a peaceful cabin in the woods of west Redding. I like to make it a practice to go away into nature to reflect on the passing year and the one approaching. For three days reading, journaling and having conversations with God were my focus. As I read Brené Brown's book *The Gifts of Imperfection* I experienced an epiphany that changed my self view forever.

What I came to realise was I had been living with the

'Ghastly Twins' - Shame & Guilt. Somehow through-out my life I believed myself to be a bad person. Up until the point of reading the book, what I didn't realise was, that the thought process followed me throughout my life; stemming from a rather colourful adolescence.

The way it showed up was constant second guessing, not trusting myself overthinking my motives and not pursuing friendships because I was convinced people didn't like me, or at least, they wouldn't like me if they got close to my heart.

The stark distinction that Brené made, literally rearranged my thinking. Through life experiences I convinced myself that I was not a good person, but the truth was I had simply made some poor choices and those choices did not define me.

I attempted to convince myself that what Brené said couldn't possibly be true, because, let's face it, what would I do with not being who I thought I was all these years? Shifting to a new truth can be scary and hard to accept sometimes, but you have to suck it up and do it. So of course, I was faced with resistance to what I read. I heard (who I refer to as) God ask me to "find"

"Shifting to a new truth can be scary and hard to accept sometimes, but you have to suck it up and do it."

evidence that supports me being a bad person. For about five minutes I tried to come up with instances that proved my point, but to no avail. From then on out I resolved and accepted that I had been carrying shame on my back most of my life and the day had come for me to be free from it.

Shame has the ability to suppress who we are. Shame has a tendency to make us feel as though we need to hide and isolate ourselves. I wish I could tell you that I don't have challenges with shame from time to time, however I do. What I can tell you is that I am lightening speeds faster at shifting my thoughts and silencing the 'reporter' in my head. I am reminded when I do something wrong, privately or publicly, not to agree with shame because that is not who I am. I take a moment to share some self-compassion, forgive and make a note to self, to do better next time and not to repeat the behaviour then keep it moving. It is a lot more empowering than the immobilising negative self-talk.

My questions for you:

1. When do thoughts of being bad or not good enough show up in your life?

2. How long do you entertain them?

3. What is your game plan for success when they surface again?

FOUR

Self - Forgiveness

"Forgiveness is inherently powerful enough to extend itself wholly and completely to us even when we are the ones in need of forgiving ourselves."
— Craig D. Lounsbrough

Often when we think of forgiveness, we think of forgiving a person for what they have done to us. It's not an immediate or co-thought that it also applies to ourselves personally. Very rarely do we make it a practice to forgive the things that we have done to ourselves. We can go through life being angry, thinking lowly of ourselves and not understanding why or how we have got to a particular place. I want to propose a question to you; Could it be your inability to forgive yourself that is keeping you a prisoner? Kris Vallotton, an incredible teacher, says that "if someone does something to us we become the victim of that persons actions. Their action has caused us to become 'captive' to the experience. As a captive, our emotions have been confined."

"When we choose to have self compassion and forgive ourselves, we empower who we are."

When we know that we are to 'forgive' the person for their actions and we don't, we have voluntarily chosen to become a 'prisoner' to the situation.

We need to learn to be able to relate that principle back to ourselves, with us being the antagoniser. Imagine, we are going about our day and something serious occurs. Our inner thoughts become negative, we may even say something verbally about ourselves. When this happens and is repeated, we are creating a personal history that in turn is telling our heart what we think of it.

When this happens, we break down trust with ourselves, that has potential to take us to a place we would prefer not to be. You may be in that place now. I understand that it can be hard to forgive ourselves for an action(s) that we may have committed to ourselves, and especially difficult if others were affected by our decision. I would like to share some good news, forgiveness can be a process. I've found that the more we extend self-compassion, the easier it becomes. I know sometimes there are pressures to think that forgiveness is something that can happen at the snap of a finger, however I haven't found that to be true in many circumstances. The truth is, when we choose to have self compassion and forgive ourselves, we empower who we are. We will be kinder to our hearts and love ourselves a lot more as we walk in authenticity.

My questions for you:

1. What things have you not forgiven yourself for yet?

2. What steps can you take to help move you towards forgiveness?

3. How will you know when self-forgiveness has happened?

FIVE

Compassionate Leave

Definition: A period or absence from work, granted to someone as a result of personal particular circumstances.

Another insight anchor I've discovered in living authentically is having a healthy level of self-compassion. This has helped me to no end and has aided me to own my truth and my story. Dr Kristin Neff, a self-compassion researcher defines self-compassion through three main components – self-kindness, common humanity, and mindfulness.

- Self-kindness: Being warm towards oneself when encountering pain and personal shortcomings, rather than ignoring them or hurting oneself with self-criticism.

- Common humanity: Self-compassion also involves recognizing that suffering and personal failure is a part of the shared human experience.

- Mindfulness: Taking a balanced approach to one's negative emotions so that feelings are neither suppressed nor exaggerated. Negative thoughts and emotions are observed with openness, so that they are held in mindful awareness. Mindfulness is a nonjudgmental, receptive mind state in which individuals observe their thoughts and feelings as they are, without trying to suppress or deny them.

Until I discovered Dr. Neff, I had not thought about self compassion. The thought and expression for compassion towards others, yes, but toward myself wasn't something that I'd consciously made a decision to do. This was another concept that transformed my relationship with myself. If you find that you become critical for things that you have said or done, you may want to take the self compassion test on Dr. Neff's website: www.self-compassion.org

I was surprised when I got the results and realised that I needed to stop punishing myself for the things that I deemed as "stupid". Isn't it interesting how much easier it is to act in kindness towards other people who may have made the same mistakes or decisions that we have, but rarely extend that love to ourselves?

Sorry to pop your bubble darling, but we will never have everything "all together" all the time. Life just doesn't happen that way. The reality is, we are all going to fail at some point. We will discover things that we don't like about ourselves, but in those times how we treat ourselves is important.

If our friend fails in something that they have attempted, I would hope that our response is one of kindness towards them. In the same way, learning to personally adopt these practices ought to become a staple in the relationship we nurture with ourselves. When we take a step back from a particular behaviour and ask questions like '"why do you think you did that?'" and 'Where did that thought process/behaviour come from?'" we begin to understand the WHY behind the WHAT of what we've done. I've found that with understanding comes the power to proactively change that thought processes, actions or behaviours without casting self-shame.

Self-compassion is acting with kindness towards yourself when you are having a difficult time, fail or notice something you don't like about yourself. Instead of just ignoring your pain with a "stiff upper lip" mentality, you stop to tell yourself "this is really difficult right now, how can I comfort and care for

"Self-compassion is acting with kindness towards yourself."

you in this moment?" I entitled this insight 'Compassionate Leave' because many of us need to take leave from beating ourselves up for the things that we have done. What tends to happen for a majority of people is we hold ourselves at an unrealistically high standard and become hostage to it. Please do not get me wrong, having high standards is a good thing, however we must ensure that we have them in the right context for their execution.

When our self-compassion muscle is developed, our default setting will be the choice to be kind to ourselves, and to stop putting unnecessary pressure and expectations on our lives. Governing our treatment towards our heart keeps our hearts cared for and feeling loved by us - it's owner - which in turn will serve us with love and self-acceptance while embracing beautiful change as we proactively and kindly work on our areas needing improvement!

My questions for you:

1. What does your internal voice tell you when you do something you deem as wrong?

2. How much self-compassion do you have? Tip: Do the test!

3. What can you do to increase your compassion levels? Tip: Do Dr Neff's exercises.

SIX

Emotional Honesty

honest

ˈɒnɪst/

adjective

adjective: honest

1. free of deceit; truthful and sincere.

2. truthful, sincere, candid, frank, direct, open, forthright, straight, straightforward, genuine, blunt, plain-spoken, plain-speaking, matter-of-fact, outspoken, as straight as a die, straight from the shoulder;

One of the most challenging things to do is to be honest with our emotions. Before we can be honest, we have to understand and accept our emotions are perfectly OK to have. Have you ever seen a person who is happy but somehow has forgotten to tell their face? Being sincere and speaking our truth (with honour) can be challenging for various reasons, however it is one of the most freeing things we could ever do.

'"How is your heart doing?"

"Excuse me? What does that even mean?"

We must own our emotional state and emotions, or how else will we process them when they surface? Imagine a sponge that has water in it, from a distance you can't really tell that it contains water until it has been squeezed. In the same manner, if we do not connect with and process our emotions honestly when pressure comes, they will show up and show outwardly. Addressing our emotions safeguards us from creating a sense of numbness and creates a personal history that communicates to our hearts that it is valuable.

"How is your heart doing? Excuse me? What does that even mean?"

I remember when someone asked me that question, I thought the person was loony! How could I possibly know how my heart was doing, who has ever heard of such a thing!?

I was encouraged to use the method of asking my heart how it is, and what it needs. I know, it sounds bizarre but I've made it a practice and it's helped me to love myself the way my heart needs me to. Let me tell you a story... In 2013, my father transitioned from this earth. As he lay on the bed I made a conscious decision to speak to my heart - "Heart, we are not going to "numb out", I promise to allow you to express your emotions whenever you need, and wherever we are". Making that decision at that critical time has helped immensely with grieving.

What that did was create a space to embrace emotion and ride its wave that would inevitably show up. In choosing authenticity, I armed myself with knowing that I do not have to "put on a front", have it "all together" or be "strong for my family". When we allow our hearts to freely express itself we are saying "you are worthy of being heard and I want to hear what you have to say".

Have you ever had a conversation with someone where you walk away thinking "ugh, I should have said xyz?" Or have you been in a conversation and at that moment you know what you want to say, but for whatever reason you choose not to? Then for the rest of the week, that silenced comment keeps plaguing you. Yep! May I propose, that is your heart telling you that you hadn't given it the value that it needed - that value that says your "voice" counts? Being honest with our emotions gives us and the people we trust the chance to see and know us deeper. When you're truthful about what you're experiencing without sugar coating it (around the right people) we will find an ear to listen or a shoulder to cry on if we need it - and at some point we all do.

You may say "I don't get emotional", but I'd like to propose, that is not normal. Some people are afraid of their emotions, locking them away in a secure box and storing it in a basement of their life. The more we acknowledge and stay true to our emotions, the more we grow in authenticity, firstly to ourselves and then to those around us.

My questions for you:

1. How is your heart doing?

2. What does it need right now? e.g.. Time out, social time, to verbally process.

3. What things can you do to cultivate a better relationship with your heart?

SEVEN

Acknowledge Your Emotions

"Emotions are good indicators, sign posting you to
what's going on in your heart."
- Cherlene Wilson

In May 2013 when my father passed away, waves
of grief would find me. "Will I embrace the wave or
fight it?" Mr Mc aka "my dad" as I affectionately
called him, was an incredibly funny man! Many times
sharing jokes with an expressionless face. He was a
man of principle, and ever so proud of his Jamaican
heritage the phrase "missing him" will never suffice.
My Dad transitioned at 7:30am on a Sunday
morning. That very evening I was standing in
character in a theatre production, in front of an

audience of 200, as a mentally challenged, heroine and alcohol addict who was a mother to a teenage girl. The performance was spectacular and one of my all time favourite acting experiences to date. What no one saw was the tears back stage between parts, the extreme focus to not forget my lines and composing myself as I stepped into a coffin (yes, you read right) for the play's closing scene.

For the next month my body experience extreme trauma, where my menstrual cycle showed up unexpectedly and remained for 31 days. At the time of writing this very line, it is 3 years on from that day. As the time has gone by I have learnt that choosing to acknowledge my emotions is critical for emotional health and stewarding authenticity, with myself and people around me.

Learning that our emotions are good indicators, but not good decision makers, has been a lifeline and motivation, to do my best to be keep mobilised. It is important that we

"Choosing to acknowledge emotions is critical in stewarding authenticity."

keep short accounts with ourselves, on the way that we feel. I have found that by valuing my emotions, even if I don't have all language for it I can still remain true to being honest with myself.

I found that the mere fact of acknowledging something is not quite right, can aide in the discovery of the root of that feeling. It is easy for us to inadvertently be unaware of our feelings as we are consumed with day to day tasks. In that, it may be a good idea for us to factor in a time to draw out our emotions throughout the day. Have conversations with yourself, "self how are you feeling today?" is a great start! Journaling is a good way to monitor how you're feeling, some people write at the start and/or end of their day. Find what works for you and add it to your authenticity tool box.

My questions for you:

1. What good/bad emotions are you avoiding?

2. How can you become more aware of your emotions?

3. How can you effectively manage your emotions at the same time as honouring them?

EIGHT

Self-Awareness

"He who knows others is wise. He who knows himself is enlightened."
- Lao Tzu

I remember when one of my teachers at the leadership school I attended told me that at times I walked around like a storm. If I was upset, apparently everyone knew about it. The atmosphere would shift. Err! Really? I was oblivious! A friend told me that I need to smile more because I constantly look upset! What!!? I'm not upset all the time! Perhaps I needed to tell my face that! The truth was I couldn't see outside the world that I had created for myself. I wasn't aware of how my behaviour and attitude could impact the people around me. Over the course of time I began to be more sensitive to it. I did an Assessment 360 where you have your closest friends answer specific questions. Boy was I nervous of what my friends would say when I sent them the document. The good news is my friends were brutally honest. At this point I was a few years on from my teachers' comment. The report came back almost 100% sparkling, I was very surprised.

To be our true authentic self takes for us to be aware of our thoughts as what we think inevitably becomes our actions. We need to understand our strengths and weaknesses - this helps us to understand where we shine and what we need help with, rather than pretending "to be" and struggle with areas which we honestly end up wasting time on.

"I think self-awareness is probably the most important thing towards being a champion."
- Billie Jean King

We are all destined to be champions of our lives. Our lives are destined for greatness! The more aware we become, the more we can walk in our true power; the power to be. Our souls depend on it! Can you imagine what your life would be like if you peeled back your the power of negative life experiences, limiting beliefs, and anything that holds you back? As I write this I see you and I standing in front of each other in the stance of Superman as he grips and tears his clothes to reveal the big red and yellow 'S' (of course for us ladies ours would be encrusted with diamonds). I see the outer garments as all things negative and the inside glowing with pure white! That glow lives inside of us! Some see it more than others. Some can feel it in there but need help to let it shine. Wherever you are on that spectrum, the reality is, you were created to shine and shine bright! Let us forever be on a quest to be true to ourselves.

My questions for you:

1. How can you grow in self-awareness?

2. Who can you ask about how you affect your
    environment?

3. When will you ask them?

NINE

Apology? I am who I am!

"Imperfections are <u>not</u> inadequacies; they are
reminders that we're all in this together."
- Dr Brené Brown

Have you ever found yourself apologising for who
you are? I have, it may not have been out loud with
words, but reflected through my behaviour and
thought processes. I would think that I was "in the
way" or the classic - if someone was unhappy about
something (as I perceived it). I would believe that I
was the cause of the issue and of course I was
sorry! I would excuse myself from scenarios or
listen to voices that tried to convince me that I
wasn't being myself. I remember on one occasion I
was with a group of friends. I felt in a particularly
geeky mood and started down 'geek avenue'. Later

that day someone I was with commented rather sharply that I was trying to be someone I was not. As a result, I became super conscious and chose to suppress my 'cray cray' for many years!

What happened in that scenario? Rather than dismiss the statement as that person's view, I allowed it to determine how I would behave from there on out. I gave their opinion more value and power than my own. Have you done that before? It took a number of years to "behave" my way out, to remove that lie out of my system and to be comfortable with showing that side of me in public again. If I could speak to my 20 something self I would have said, "Do you boo! You are who you are, you don't ever have to apologise for that!" I want you to think about this for a moment - have you or are you suppressing who you are because of what someone has said? Is it possible you are communicating to yourself that who you are is not ok? Is it possible that as a result of self-editing, people are being robbed of the delight that you are?

I'm aware that people may feel that what I'm saying here gives licence to be obnoxious - that's what I don't mean. What I'm saying is, there are people across the globe who are not "our flavour"...and that's ok! In the same manner we won't be other

"Opinions may be had, but the greatest and most important opinion is the one that you have of yourself."

people's "flavour". Opinions may be had, but the greatest and most important opinion is the one that you have of yourself. It will empower you to not be ashamed or embarrassed by who you are but to fully embrace you in your entirety.

No one has it all together. Like yourself, love yourself, look in the mirror and be proud of who you are at this very moment reading this! You are who you are now, there will always be room for improvement - in your evolving, love you!

My questions for you:

1. What environments do you edit yourself in? i.e.. work, home, business.

2. What in particular do you find yourself apologising for?

3. What (positive) opinions you have of yourself? If you don't have any, make them up!

I am_____

I am_____

I am_____

TEN

Understanding Your Uniqueness

"To be yourself in a world that is constantly trying to make you something else is the greatest accomplishment."
— Ralph Waldo Emerson

Each person embodies uniqueness incomparable to any one on the planet. Our gifts, talents, multiple intelligences, areas of interest, experiences, strengths, weaknesses etc - all contribute to being an individual gift wrapped in skin with a mandate to serve the world.

It is what makes the world as colourful, fun and interesting as it is. In my experience of coaching clients, I have learnt that very rarely do they know, or feel comfortable to voice and accept their own uniqueness! On my personal journey from self-hatred to self-love, one of the most profound things that I have learnt is how external testing can help. It can confirm or shine light on what we may already know to be true about ourselves and/or highlight aspects that have gone unnoticed. We've all seen those fun tests on social media where we answer questions that tell us what country we would be best suited to live in - Although fun, and at times accurate, those are not the kinds of tests I mean.

I have done quite a few tests in my lifetime which have helped undergird my understanding of who I am, and affirm some aspects of my uniqueness. One of the tests that we were asked to do as part of my leadership school class was *Strength Finder 2.0* by Tom Rath and oh my goodness! To learn of my strengths and how they play out in my life gave me such confidence because I was already living them, but just didn't know they were strengths. This new level of raised awareness complimented and confirmed what I already knew I was talented in, creatively and professionally. It took me a while to be ok with the fact that I'm dramatic. Let me be clear I don't mean I'm drama, I mean dramatic in my expression of things! I used to assign negative connotations to it, until I chose to define it myself - yes I took the power of redefining what I wanted 'drama' to mean. There have been times, where friends, family and I have been left laughing about the idiosyncrasies of Cherlene Wilson. It's beautiful, it is simply just me. Friends may say "you're special" and you just have to reply with "you're right!"

There will never ever be anyone exactly like us on the earth so being authentic in who we are is something we ought to delight in as we live our lives daily. When we know who we are and embrace our personality, we can show up in a room without the need to feel like we have to 'edit' ourselves to satisfy the environment.

Of course depending on our environment we may need to *adapt* ourselves and display the etiquette needed, but that is very different from editing the core of who we are to be accepted.

I am passionate about people discovering the intricate details of their

"When we know who we are and embrace our personality, we can show up in a room without the need to feel like we have to "edit" ourselves to satisfy the environment".

Personalities, because it helped me to 'show up' and love myself for who I am, when self-hate was tangible in my life. This is the same reason I became a Personality Analyst. I'm sure new friends and old ones get driven up the wall as I analyse them, assessing if they are an introvert or extrovert, what their Myers-Briggs acronym. And whether they are a D, i, S or C personality blend is; but it's a passion for me to know people and for them to also learn new things about themselves.

It's especially fun to see the expression on new people's faces when I ask them if they are like XYZ and they exclaim, "yes, how did you know that!?" It's a beautiful thing to see as they learn that it is ok to be who they are - self acceptance in action! I think it is critical that we are acutely aware of what makes us unique. I believe, that as we grow in authenticity that we make it a common practice to take the time to learn about the person we will spend the rest of our lives living with - ourselves.

My questions for you:

1. Do you know how you are uniquely wired?

2. List 3 quirks that make you unique?

3. Are you an "editor" or "adapter", how self aware are you in various environments? Take notes from now on.

ELEVEN

The Core of Who You Are

"Your core values are the deeply held beliefs that
authentically describe your soul."
- John C. Maxwell

At some point in our lives, we will ask ourselves
that sobering question: "who am I?" We will arrive at
this question some way or another - perhaps due to
frustration, or surprise from an awesome self
discovery. Throughout our lives we may have been
told who we are, based on the perception and
opinion of others, however rarely ask ourselves who
we believe we truly are. Understanding and
embracing our core self is critical to our
authenticity journey.

The core self is the centre-point of where all your decisions are made, one could say your internal identification system. Imagine an apple, you have the flesh of the apple that we bite into - that representing external factors, i.e.. Peoples ideas, thoughts perceptions, the things around you etc. The core of the apple where the seeds reside is your core-self and where your core values live. Our core is where we contain the potential to grow into someone fruitful (cheesy I know!).

"The core self is the centre-point of where all your decisions are made."

We must know who we are, and what kind of person we are, to truly feel and display authenticity. If we do not, we allow people in our environment to do it for us, and be "blown in the wind" of people's opinions.

When we are able to identify and explain our nature, our core self - it is much easier to navigate through life and the world around us. We will have a better idea of what is right for us, just as much as what isn't right for us too.

With our core value lens, we are more likely to identify the course of our lives and correctly view the opportunities that come our way! Defining who you are is a process. It will be a technical, emotional, and interrogatory challenge. It is essential however that we know what drives us, from the inside out. A core value is a value that you have that answers a question before it has been asked. For example if your core value is 'I will use my voice for inspiration', anything opposed to that i.e. gossip or using harsh words towards another would be a lot less likely to happen.

Each one of us governs our lives through what we deem as valuable to us. Whether we identify it or not, core values are governing our lives everyday. The key is that we consciously decide on - what those positive life-giving values are, how they define us and allow them to form within our lives. To start If it hasn't happened already, we have to drill down to our fundamental self. Our fundamental self is defined as "a central or primary rule or principle on which something is based". That *something* being our lives and the way we live.

As a module in one of my coaching programs, identifying one's core values is one of the first things my clients will do. When these are defined, essentially what we are saying is, "these set of values is how I define the core of who I am and I make my decisions based on those." When we have a healthy outlook on who we are, it is much easier of us to accept ourselves. When we are authentic with wherever we are in our process, we can choose to embrace the 'now' of who we are that resonates with our soul.

When we fully subscribe to who we believe ourselves to be, we will walk in a level of authenticity and power that is contagious. We will have a level of confidence about us and have an open heart to embrace the people around us.

My questions for you:

1. What are some of your core values that govern your life?

2. What core values can you add to your life this year?

3. When will you do that?

TWELVE

Give Yourself Permission to Change

"Dream and give yourself permission to envision a
you that you choose to be."
- Joy Page

The title may sound contradictory to 'The Core Of
Who You Are', where we spoke about core values
and how they help govern our lives. The context of
'change' that we are speaking about in this insight
is the enhancement of who you are. For example:
career, hobbies and interests.

I speak with people who are unfulfilled. They are not
doing anything that makes their heart come alive.
They know that they want to engage in something

new, but there is an underpinning belief that they can't do it.

If our minds have been conditioned to believe that we must be the master of one thing and one thing alone, when our soul discovers something that makes it come alive in a way never experienced before, we have a tendency to question whether or not we should do it. For example, your career. You may have had a particular job for years, however over time (or through self-discovery) you learnt that your heart has become awakened to something else that also gives you greater satisfaction. You may think 'I couldn't possibly do that, everyone knows me as _____ (fill in the blank).' The truth is that the bridge between who you are today, and the enhancement of who you want to become tomorrow is giving yourself permission

I remember a time when I consciously felt my mind evolving. The desire for more developing, the desire to see dreams come true; new interests and dreams, like spoken word poetry and working in countries around the world. There was a problem, I saw myself as the person that I was in that moment and wondered "who do I think I am to want to be different?" I felt like going against the grain would be uncomfortable and perhaps I wouldn't be liked because of it (that 'fear of man again'). Often we think of all the opposing monumental reasons why change would be so challenging, however at the same time your soul aches to become what it sees itself to be. You may know what I'm talking about, you may be feeling this right now.

Darling, people may look at you and give you the "side eye". You may even get the odd comment about "who do you think you are", but the truth is that the opinion of the critic doesn't matter. What matters is that you "stay in your lane" and remain true to who you are. If someone opposes us for changing for the better, it tells us more about their state of being and ability to dream than it does about ours. Selah (think about it).

By the time the majority of my clients make an enquiry about working with me, they are ready for a transformational shift in their life. They feel like they are living in a mental space that

'What matters is that you "stay in your lane" and remain true to who you are."

says "There has to be more to me. Something needs to change or I'm going to continue to feel stuck in this cycle". The discomfort experienced from not being who you truly are, has to be greater than the complacency or mediocre lifestyle you have become accustomed to. Sometimes we make decisions in a particular way, yet later we realise that actually we believe new things or are no longer satisfied with a particular facet of our personality. For example, It's OK to change it, reform it, reform you! The bridge between who we are today and who we want to be tomorrow is giving ourselves permission to become that individual.

My questions for you:

1. What significant area of your life do you want to change?

2. What has stopped you from changing it so far?

3. Moving forward how will you change it and when will you start?

THIRTEEN

Making The Necessary Adjustments

"Sometimes things happen, and the only choice you have is to accept it, and learn to make a life anyway."
— M.A. McRae

Picture a sailboat, with tall mast and big sails soaring across the ocean. It is free, gently sailing in the direction of the sailor's intent! The winds change and the sails need an adjustment to ensure the boat stays on the course of the compass. Now imagine heavy winds begin to blow, the sailor runs over to the main mast, shouts out "free the sails". He grips the shroud, pulling the cable to adjust the sails then shouts to the second sailor to steer the boat via the rudder. The adjustments that have been made are to ensure that the boat can endure the winds. Two things could happen in this scenario. The boat will either be sailing against the wind or towards the wind, whatever the case, if the adjustments were not made, the boat could capsize! I believe our lives are very similar to this situation. We are all heading somewhere. Whether sailing with intention or just cruising, one thing for sure is at some point we will come up against opposing "elements" as we travel to our destination(s).

"You can allow ego and complacency to hold you back or you can jump up, adjust, using the tweaking to your advantage."

Adjusting has been one of the most challenging things for me personally in terms of personal development. I've found this especially challenging when I can sense that there is a "season shift" in my life that requires more of me. Perhaps this has happened or is happening to you. For me, it has been new opportunities that have encapsulated my hopes and desires. However, to take them I would have to step out and show up. The realisation of 'wow, in order for me to show up as my best self in that situation, I would need to develop areas in my life and face what actually needs growth'. Scary. Examples of this can be:

1. Becoming disciplined in a particular area(s)
2. Learn a skill set
3. Let some things go

When we do this, we are remaining true to what our inner-self requires from us and choosing to move with our winds of destiny.

My questions for you:

1. List three adjustments you need to make this week.

2. Put them in order with the most urgent first.

3. Find someone to hold you accountable to it.

FOURTEEN

Adapting to Your Season

"Step back in perspective, open your heart and welcome transition into a new phase of life."
— Linda Rawson

Have you ever thought of your life in seasons? Just like our natural seasons we all have seasons in our lives. Perhaps a season of education, self-discovery, learning about a particular area of relationships etc. We have to be true to our season. There are times when we just can't figure out why we feel 'out of sorts' or why things are not in flow. It is likely that you are in a new season and what worked before, may not work quite as well in the transition. If you are currently in spring, you are not going to want to show up in winter clothes because people will look at you sideways.

Have you ever felt like your levels of tolerance or patience are running thin or completely out? You see many 'signs', but choose to - for whatever reason - ignore them. That agitation will continue until you recognise it and flow with it. When we push back on the season change, we will find that we are choosing to not "show up" to the new shift in our life. We then, in essence would be living in-authentically to our season and become frustrated with ourselves, relatives and even work.

It is important that we choose to discover and understand where we're at so that we can remain authentic to our lives, to our work on the planet and of course, our destiny. In every season, we are empowered with what we will need to adapt and function within. The key here is to not resist but to roll with it.

In December of 2015 and for three months preceding I lived within a brand new continent, language and culture. It was an incredible shift in seasons (quite literally) and one that I had all of 96 hours to prepare for.

The learning curve was steep, and the culture shock very real when I arrived in Kotoko International Airport in Accra, Ghana. According to the natives my adjustment happened surprisingly fast, with many unable to identify that I was from another country. A lot was accomplished in three months, and although there were some challenging moments, all in all the 'shift with the season' was so worth it.

"Let us not be guilty of living faithfully in winter when spring has arrived."

I want you to think about your life, and where it is at now. Are you in, or do you need a shift to get you to the next season of your life? I'm not saying that you need to move to a new continent for the transition. What I am saying is that there are prompts in our lives that we need to pay attention to so we can identify when we need to adapt and live empowered in the new phase of our life, whatever that may be. Let us not be guilty of living faithfully in winter when spring has arrived.

Even though it may be scary, choose to 'show up' in your new season! Embrace and adapt to the shift. Who knows when you go with the flow, the season may surprise you and overturn your fears and exceed your expectations.

My questions for you:

1. What season of your life are you in right now?

2. Where can you feel your heart directing you to go?

3. What needs to happen for you to fully adapt to your season?

FIFTEEN

Protect Your Heart

"Above all else guard your heart, for everything you do flows from it."
- King Solomon

The amount of people that tell me they have no idea what protecting their heart means, continues to astonish to me! Now, hear me out for a second. I'm aware you may be one of those people, so let me explain.

Once upon a time, I had no idea what it meant or what the practicalities were for it either. What astonishes me is why this fails to be a staple in secondary school curriculum. Our heart is our most valuable possession, learning how to guard it in a healthy way is critical for us to turn up in the world.

"Walls are mainly used to keep things out, whereas a boundary gives access and communicates the limitations and value."

To guard our heart is to protect it from anything that could potentially cause harm to it. For years, 'protecting my heart' looked like not letting anyone come close to it! What was interesting was, I lived that way and was so unaware. Protecting the heart was a secondary consequence of previous life events, and mostly motivated by fear of being hurt or taken advantage of. What I didn't know was that the wall that I erected to protect me, was the same wall that restricted me from expressing love or receiving love the way I naturally wanted to. Perhaps that is something you may be able to relate to?

Let me ask you this: when you think of 'protecting your heart', what comes to mind? A wall? A boundary? There is a clear distinction between a wall and a boundary. Walls are mainly used to keep things out, whereas a boundary gives access and communicates the limitations and value. I feel like in order to protect our hearts well, it is imperative we have self-awareness and put out walls that shut off.

From personal experiences, we need to develop sensitivity to what our heart needs - another anchor point of living authentically. Protecting our hearts can take the shape of many different forms. An example of this was my choice to remain offline on social media (Facebook) for a number of weeks. My heart was exposed to horrendous and tragic events around the world, coupled with distasteful comments from individuals who were adding fuel to the fire of an already emotionally hostile environment. I could consciously feel my heart growing numb. I could see my view of life changing, and felt some emotions that were foreign to my heart's orientation.

One day I concluded that in order to manage my heart well, I have to stop exposing it to things that could make it sick. The 'time out' was one of the best decisions I've made. That was protecting the heart in action. Being self-aware on what can leave your heart feeling vulnerable is a great skill to have. This in turn will prompt the heart to grow in its capacity to fully function, and freely express itself with less congestion.

In our quest to freely love and be authentic in our environment, knowing that we are powerful people that govern our heart will help us live powerfully and free. Most of us have been hurt throughout our lives, and it does take intentionality to not allow that to dictate how we love.

There is a tension between creating boundaries to protect our heart and shutting off our hearts to receive the expressions of love. If we've been hurt before, we know how much of a challenge it is to open up again, and understandably so. However, we must ensure that as we develop our emotional intelligence; to be healthy wholehearted individuals, that we be mindful to know the difference between the two.

My questions for you:

1. Would you say you put up walls or boundaries around your heart?

2. What do you fear concerning matters of your heart?

3. Do you need to do any heart work? If so, what and when will you take the first step to doing it?

SIXTEEN

Brave Communication

"Good communication is just as stimulating as
black coffee, and just as hard to sleep after."
- Anne Morrow Lindbergh

I clearly remember the day when I learnt about
brave communication from one of my teachers in
leadership school. I was mesmerised by what
seemed to be a new dialect, and one that my soul
was compelled to understand.

Staging a confrontation, with the goal to create a
connection, was "other worldly" to me and
something that completely shifted my paradigm.
Effectively communicating when something was
unclear, invoked a strong emotional reaction from
me, and made me feel uncomfortable. It wasn't

something strategically thought about but rather a reactionary side-effect, combined with inflammatory language and the inability to hear what was really being said.

From my childhood, a 'normal' confrontation within my family easily resulted in disconnection, sometimes for a while, but with extended friends and family it tended to be indefinitely. This was a learnt trait on both sides of the family, going back to my grandparents. The tone for confrontation was set and the inevitable outcome would be me being 'cut off' and out of people's lives.

This topic is multi-layered and would take much longer than a chapter to remotely exhaust, so the aspect I would like to highlight is the 'I' message.

The day I learnt this message it was weirdly empowering, completely refreshing and petrifying all at the same time. It taught me how to own and express my feelings and share my needs, whilst not attacking or demanding the individual to adjust their behaviour and/or words in the process. Then the day came, a day for me to use what I learnt. I still chuckle at the memory of saying it while my heart was pounding out of my chest, "brave communication actually requires me to have courage and be brave!" It just didn't occur to me at the time.

In order of us to be authentic with ourselves and others, expressing our hearts is imperative. When we choose to own our emotions, at best we are honouring and loving ourselves while giving the person we are speaking to information on how we are feeling and what we need from them in the relationship. I remember how I would feel when I heard the words "I need to talk to you!". Already in my mind I had concluded that whatever was about to go down would surely conclude in the termination of the friendship. If not that, then deep dissatisfaction and a change in the dynamic of the relationship.

I will be honest with you, this insight has been one of the most challenging, but also one of the most rewarding. Brave communication becomes the vehicle for which courage and authenticity co-ride to create or maintain intimacy in our relationships.

It gives the receiver the opportunity to see into your heart and create trust which will ultimately breed more freedom in the relationship.

Imagine how vulnerable you would feel saying to someone "I feel like I have no voice when I'm cut off in a conversation because when I was younger I felt like my voice had no value. So, I need a chance to finish my train of thought when talking."

Can you feel the authenticity and vulnerability in that script? You can see complete ownership of emotions and what the need is. With such a clear, direct, non-confrontational approach, the receiver is given explicit information as to how their actions are affecting you and what you need from them in order for it to change.

Have you ever been in the situation where you chose not to tell someone about how you were feeling? Did negative emotions such as bitterness, anger, mistrust and avoidance began to creep in? Clearly these all undermine authentic living and can steal our relationships if we allow it to go unaddressed. With knots in our tummy and a racing pulse, validating your emotions and speaking about it, is another sure enough way to be true to your heart and who you are.

My questions for you:

1. What is your 'normal' communication?

2. What scares you the most about communicating your feelings?

3. What can you do today to improve your communication skills?

SEVENTEEN

Being True to Your Word

"Be impeccable with your word. Speak with integrity. Say only what you mean. Avoid using the word to speak against yourself or to gossip about others. Use the power of your word in the direction of truth and love."
- Don Miguel Ruiz

I was recommended Don Miguel's book *The Four Agreements*. If you are yet to read it, please put down this book and order it immediately! I felt like the first agreement - Be Impeccable with Your Word, ties into authentic living. Whether we realise it or not, our words are the vehicle that forms our lives as we create a personal history with ourselves and others. What I mean is, do what you say you're going to do.

According to Don Miguel, Impeccable means 'without sin'. WOW! Think about that for a moment! When Don Miguel speaks about words in this context, he not only means us keeping our word with others and ourselves, but also the use of our words with others and ourselves. For some of us this isn't new information, however the way in which he presented it, put a new spin on it for me.

When we don't keep our word with ourselves and others, we eat away at our soul and break down the level of trust that we have in ourselves. How do you build trust with people? It's through relationship, experiences and showing through various acts that you are trustworthy. In the same way, in one of the greatest relationships we have (the relationship with ourselves), we ought to strive to create that same type of trust. Have you found yourself thinking or feeling like you don't trust your judgment or what you say you are going to do? Have you felt like you need to go to multiple people to get their 'opinion" on everything and then decide? May I propose that it is highly likely that your personal history of trust needs to be looked at?

What words are we using in our internal world? Is it possible that they are breaking down our infrastructure?

"Our choice of words becomes an extension of who we are, what we think in our mind and the foundation of how we form our lives."

Have you ever had one of those instances where follow through has not happened yet, and then that sinking feeling in the gut starts to happen: "I wasn't true to what I said I'd do". You walk around feeling 'blah', and work on making it up, whether that is to yourself or to someone else. Yes! We all have. Also have you had that feeling where you do what you say you were going to do and feel like a champion on top of the world!? Yes! We all have. Not to say there won't be times when we are unable to fulfill our agreement, however that ought to be less of a practice and more of an exception to the rule.

Our choice of words becomes an extension of who we are, what we think in our mind and the foundation of how we form our lives. So we must be mindful in their use. Don Miguel, refers to negative words, i.e. gossip and words used at people as 'black magic'. This means negative words release poison into the person if that person agrees with what is being said about them. Those words could very much be the cause of keeping people confined within poisonous situations - because of what was said to them and in turn choosing to agree with it.

He also spoke about words that are positive and uplifting, labelling those as 'white magic'. He has selected the word 'magic' to illustrate the power of words. Just like a 'magic trick', one minute something is the way you see it, then the next thing you know, "Voilá!" it has changed. In the same way our words are powerful to shift atmospheres in ourselves and others.

Let us look at our lives and how we use our words. Let us be mindful and speak with integrity. Saying what we mean, and meaning what we say. As people, let our nature be to love and connect with each other, lifting each other up and cheering one another on. Let us be "without sin" and create/maintain a history of being true to our word.

My questions for you:

1. What areas of our relationship with self do you need to improve with your words?

2. What areas of your life do you need to develop self-trust?

3. What relationships do you need to have more integrity in?

EIGHTEEN

Saying 'Hello' to Vulnerability

"To share your weakness is to make yourself
vulnerable; to make yourself vulnerable is to show
your strength."
— Criss Jami

Vulnerability wasn't something I felt could be a
choice. Perhaps that's a little elementary for some,
however personally, feeling vulnerable was always
as result of someone else's actions. I learnt (as a
by-product) that it was important for me to protect
myself from any possible danger - albeit
hypothetical. All that did was sabotage my
relationships. When genuine love (platonic or

romantic) was expressed, it was a challenge to fully accept it as genuine.

Throughout my journey of self-development I learnt I could choose vulnerability and choose to allow safe people into the very deep places of my heart. Now I'll say this - sharing your weaknesses, the things that are going on in your heart right now, is not for the faint-hearted. You will wonder "why the heck am I doing this?" It could scare you to your core, depending on how far removed you are from the need to be loved and accepted.

"Each one of us owe it to ourselves to master - what seems to be the art of vulnerability!"

Recently I had an 'episode'. This was season 36 episode 4! I made a decision and I needed to speak with my girls - the besties! I was in what seemed like an internal battle with myself and I needed peace. Before I texted my friend to let her know I need to talk to her and Lauren, my heart raced! "Will it be too emotional?" "Maybe, just maybe they'll think I'm just over emotional!" Either way, I was going in! What was my safety net? I knew that they loved and accepted me - regardless. I was weak, I was scared, but I knew that in that vulnerable place, because of who they were - I'd be perfectly safe. They were gentle with my heart (as I knew they would be), helped me to identify some things and even fully supported my desire to do a symbolic act to release some things from my heart! That event...actually occurred the day I wrote this insight. It's been 10 hours after the dramatics, I felt stronger. There was something in my weakness that gave birth to greater strength. The vulnerability pulled our heart strings a lot tighter together and the feeling of closeness has deepened. Each one of us owe it to ourselves to master - what seems to be the art of vulnerability! The first time I heard the phrase in-to-me-see (intimacy), was from one of my mentors, Danny Silk. What? In-to-who-see-what?! If intimacy is scary for you (I don't mean sexual intimacy) you may have thought the same thing. Regardless of who we are, we all have a desire to be completely present, connected and free in our souls.

Getting to a place where I could sit down and "keep it '100%' with my girls didn't happen overnight. It was a journey, a journey to trust myself and trust them with my heart. What is my point? I've found from personal experience that living a life of authenticity largely lends itself to being vulnerable with other people and yourself.

What I would like you to do here is honestly assess how you feel about being vulnerable. What emotions are evoked, thought processes even? The "V word" can be scary, but also one of the most empowering and freeing things we could do.

My questions for you:

1. What thoughts/feeling did you have when you read the title of this chapter?

2. How do you define vulnerability?

3. What do you believe to be true if you choose to be vulnerable?

NINETEEN

"I Need You!"

"Be strong enough to stand alone, smart enough to know when you need help, and brave enough to ask for it." - Unknown

Have you ever taken a step back and realised that ego has robbed you of things in your life? Perhaps friendships, business relationships or great opportunities? Pride can be one of the most crippling aspects of an individual's character and can literally alter the course of someone's destiny.

Admitting that we don't have it 'all together' and we need the help of another person can be uncomfortable, but is one of the most freeing things to do when it comes to the topic of authenticity. "I need you", is one of the most vulnerable things to admit to a person. Let me be clear here, I'm not speaking of the unhealthy 'needy' co-dependent kind of need. I am speaking of the kind that reaches out to people that can help you with something you feel you don't have the capacity to do. I have had people message me and tell me that they would rather suffer in silence than admit to anyone that they need assistance. I understand it, but how is that working out for you in practice? At best it is slowing you down, whether that is healing to your heart, growth in our business or support in our education or day-to-day life.

"Pride and ego masks our authentic self, parading around us like a carnival of elaborate colours and verbalisations."

I don't know why this is, but for me the older I get, the more I feel like there is something that I ought to already 'know' at the age I'm at. It is one of the biggest deceptions and a 'staple' in pride and is 'game face' is put on. You try to work your way through it and it's still a challenge. Taking that 'game face' off and letting the weakness be seen is one of the most beautiful, authentic and strong things we can do.

Pride and ego masks our authentic self, parading around us like a carnival of elaborate colours and verbalisations. It's a distraction from our true selves, robbing us of a more fulfilled and authentic life. What has ego stolen from you? That friendship you valued? Disconnection from your emotions? Separation from the people you care about most? A business opportunity that had the potential of being great? Make no mistakes, we have all done this in one way or another. What needs to happen here is the appreciation that most of us want to be self-sufficient. The fact is, it's not always possible and asking for assistance doesn't make us weak but rather adds to the strength of our pre-existing selves.

My questions for you:

1. What areas of your life are you 'over' self-sufficient?

2. When have you delayed asking for help, but when you did it worked out well?

3. What did you learn about yourself in that moment?

TWENTY

Fix Your Crack

"The loftier the building, the deeper must the
foundation be laid".
- Thomas A Kempis

In 2015 I posted a quote that said "Being high
powered is one thing; but being high powered and
broken could cost you your destiny and the destiny
of others!" Prior to posting, I had been thinking
about it for quite some time. Many of us aspire to
be influential in our sphere of influence, but I have
often found that many people like to jump over the
cracks and broken parts of their lives and not take
the time to solidify the foundation. Have you done
that before? It's VERY easy to happen, I know all too
well.

"Being high powered is one thing; but being high powered and broken could cost you your destiny and the destiny of others!"

In the summer of 2016, after I had graduated my first year of ministry leadership school I was very pleased with myself. I was FULLY convinced that I was going to be back for the second year, because I was awesome! "How could I not pass my interview?" I was so confident that I left all my belongings in storage for my return that summer! Well, I had the interview for my second year and was told that I was unsuccessful! The short version of the story is that I contended the decision and was offered the opportunity to repeat first year again! Yes AGAIN! What helped me make the decision to repeat (or as I called it "extend my first year") was this.

The truth was I had some 'issues' darling! The foundation was unstable. Although I couldn't see it, it could be seen by the individuals I trusted to lead me. I had to do whatever it would take to become as whole as I could in that season of my life. Although it was painful, I said to myself "in the grand scheme of my life, to sit through another nine months to solidify my foundation would be worth it; because I know that God has a great call on my life. I would hate to reach a height of influence and come crumbling down under the pressure of it all and quite possibly taking people with me". It was a very real and humbling moment. I learnt some of the greatest lessons about myself in that time.

Some of those lessons were:

1. Taking a few steps back so you can make a running jump is wisdom.

2. Take your power and be responsible for your life.

3. Embrace the process, don't run from it.

4. Getting help to fill in the cracks is much easier than doing it on your own.

5. Asking for help isn't a sign of weakness, but rather a sign of strength.

Embrace your short-comings, and clean up the messes made throughout your life or situations that you have experienced. Do not allow things that may have broken you to remain that way! They can be fixed, for real! I can testify! Seeing who I have become because of embracing the process of change absolutely blows my mind. The same *will be* true for you!

My questions for you:

1. What cracks are you ignoring?

2. When are you going to confront them and deal with them?

3. What course of action will you take to fill them in?

TWENTY ONE

Truth Tellers

"Wounds made by a friend are intended to help, but an enemy's kisses are too much to bear."
- King Solomon

If one thing is going to help you live an authentic life, it's going to be Truth Tellers (TT"s). These are individuals that love you, care about your heart and future. These are people who are not intimidated by who you may be, your economic status or influence in society. They want the best for you! They will hold up that mirror for you, celebrate you, champion you and love you way too much to let you sit in anything that does not serve your life and the core message of who you are.

I have my inner circle and a handful of individuals around me that "just tell it as it is". I love these people, they have the loudest voice of influence in my life and I trust them to tell me the truth, they have permission to highlight any blind spots which may be good or bad things I don't see and champion me in life. My circle knows that authenticity and living a life that pursues destiny everyday is important to me. I have found myself positioning my heart to listen to theirs, to hear their opinion, think about it and make any necessary adjustments. This remains critical in my personal evolution and the speed of my growth. It keeps me accountable to the assignment on my life - my message to the world.

Knowing that their intentions are pure and they want to see me 'win' in life gives me great confidence and the inspiration to keep it moving, even when I'm at my wits end and want to disappear to an island far, far away. On one occasion, two ladies (from my inner circle) and I were hanging out at home. I don't remember how the conversation started but both of them sat with me and told me some home truths. Ouch! It was painful, but loving.

I did cry, but it was good for the soul. Having things highlighted by someone else, helped me to see what I was oblivious to and raised my awareness. The same is also true for great things. One friend has an uncanny way of summarising the things about me that I haven't realised are incredible, and bringing them to my attention! Another will sit and share at great length their observations on the lives they see impacted through interactions with me i.e. in my classes. My facial expressions always have me

The "higher" people are in their influence, the more challenging it is to find people who will straight-talk and tell them the truth.

chuckling as my already big eyes widen and the sudden awareness of "oh my gosh you're right" comes out my mouth! My friends and I often laugh about how oblivious I can be at times. What is beautiful about TT"s is that they will help you to see your greatness! This is one way that has assisted me in remaining grounded and helps me to live out my truth.

Openly inviting TT's into your life may not be something that you have ever thought about doing or even being comfortable with. If you haven't and you want/need some truth tellers maybe today is your day to think about that. I understand it may not be so easy, it may take time, but it"s worth it. I've found through my coaching career especially with celebrity and high net worth people, the 'higher' people are in their influence, the more challenging it is to find people who will straight-talk and tell them the truth.

Regardless of where or who we are, deep down in our souls we crave the truth. It's always beautiful to see people, see themselves, in ways they have never seen before. One of the greatest insights I have to share with you is this: it may take courage to give people permission to speak into your life, but it could be one of your greatest, life shifting blessings.

My questions for you:

1. Have you given people in your life permission to tell you the truth?

2. If not, what are your reasons and are they valid?

3. How frequently do/will you "check in" with them to do an assessment?

CONCLUDING THOUGHTS

It is fair to say, since you have this book in your possession, and have gotten to this page that you desire to live a more authentic life. Living authentically is a daily choice that we will need to consciously make in order for its repetition to become our reputation. It will take a continuous effort, especially when intuitively it feels safer to hide our feelings and who we are. It is necessary to embrace this as an overt way of living if we want to increase the quality and connectedness in our lives, and present our true selves.

In our quest for authenticity, knowing and fortifying our core is going to help steer our lives, driven by a confidence in who we are and who we are becoming. As we shine the light at any darkness in our souls, we will find that we will be able to own our truth and empower our stories. As we give ourselves permission to change and make the necessary adjustments, we will find that the result will be us solidifying the foundation on which our lives are built on.

"Our relationship with self is critical as we nurture self love."

As we acknowledge and understand our emotions, tapping in to self-compassion will be a calming fluid upon our hearts. It is paramount for us to be acutely aware that our relationship with self is critical as we nurture self love. The more we learn to accept ourselves, the more peace we will acquire in our internal 'world', relinquishing any desire to edit who we are, to become who we think people want or think we should be.

It is my hope that as you have read through this book (and perhaps seen some of yourself in the stories) that your heart was ignited. I hope you feel like you're not alone, and feel empowered to adopt any of the insights you may find helpful to your life.

As we journey through life, we will find more and more things that help us show up confidently. Being fully ourselves as a lifestyle, opposed to an occasion will not happen overnight, but it will happen…I promise. We must be kind to our hearts, loving ourselves the way we would love the person we love most in our lives.

What would it look like if we really presented all of who we are - a wonderful gift to the world? What would it look like if everyone chose to do just that? Confidence looks different on different people, but what would it look like if we lived our lives without apologising for who we are? Let us shine bright like that diamond Rihanna sings about!

As Marianne Williamson says:

> *"Our deepest fear is not that we are inadequate. Our deepest fear is that we are powerful beyond measure. It is our light, not our darkness that most frightens us. We ask ourselves, Who am I to be brilliant, gorgeous, talented, fabulous? Actually, who are you not to be? You are a child of God. Your playing*

small does not serve the world. There is nothing enlightened about shrinking so that other people won't feel insecure around you. We are all meant to shine, as children do. We were born to make manifest the glory of God that is within us. It's not just in some of us; it's in everyone. And as we let our own light shine, we unconsciously give other people permission to do the same. As we are liberated from our own fear, our presence automatically liberates others."

Thank you for taking the time to read this book. As we conclude, let us make this declaration:

"I am unique! I am powerful! I have a beautiful soul and I give myself permission to be who I am! Self, I accept you! I accept that I am a blessing to the world around me! Who I am right now is awesome and who I am becoming is even more awesome. I owe it to the world to show up with my unique gift mix, interests, strengths, personality and talents that are wrapped up in who I am! With all my idiosyncrasies & quirks I am loveable. Self, I love you!! We are worthy of love! We are worthy of

belonging! We will continuously practice authentic-city and find the courage to search for any darkness and empower the light, and simply BE".

CONNECT

Let us know how this book impacted you. Whether you have an eBook or paperback take a shot with/of it and post on Facebook, Instagram or Twitter with the hashtag #21InsightsCW

To have me appear at your next live event, e-mail bookings@cherlenewilson.com

www.cherlenewilson.com

Connect on social media: Facebook | Instagram | Periscope | Twitter - @cherlenewilson

CW
CHERLENE
WILSON

Printed in Great Britain
by Amazon

31646387R00073